AVIATION STORIES

FOR CURIOUS KIDS

Explore the Fascinating Tales of Airplanes, Pioneer Pilots, and Flight Mysteries!

STUART AKOLI

AVIATION STORIES

FOR CURIOUS KIDS

Explore the Fascinating Tales
of Aviation Pioneers, Firsts,
and Flight Potential

TABLE OF CONTENTS

INTRODUCTION

Welcome aboard, young aviators, to "Aviation Stories for Curious Kids"! Get ready to embark on an exhilarating journey through the captivating world of flight, where history's most daring pilots and groundbreaking aircraft await your exploration.

In this thrilling collection, we'll soar through the skies alongside legendary figures like Amelia Earhart, Charles Lindbergh, and Chuck Yeager, uncovering the secrets of their remarkable adventures. From the daring escapades of World War I flying aces to the awe-inspiring feats of modern space exploration, each story is filled with excitement, courage, and the boundless spirit of discovery.

But this isn't just a book about planes and pilots; it's a journey of curiosity and wonder. Along the way, we'll unravel mysteries like the disappearance of Amelia Earhart, the enigma of Flight 19, and the eerie phenomena of the Bermuda Triangle. We'll marvel at the ingenuity of aircraft like the Boeing 747, the Concorde, and the SR-71 Blackbird, each pushing the boundaries of what's possible in the vast expanse of the sky.

So, buckle up and prepare for takeoff as we embark on a thrilling adventure through the history of aviation. From the daring escapades of early pioneers to the groundbreaking achievements of modern technology, "Aviation Stories for Curious Kids" invites you to spread your wings and explore the wonders of flight like never before. Get ready to be inspired, amazed, and, above all, curious about the endless possibilities that await us in the boundless blue yonder.

AVIATION STORIES FOR CURIOUS KIDS

STORY 1:

Did the Wright Brothers' Homemade Plane Really Take Off?

Once upon a time, in a small town named Kitty Hawk, there were two super cool brothers named Orville and Wilbur Wright. They didn't just dream of flying; they were convinced they could do it with a sprinkle of magic and a ton of hard work.

Orville and Wilbur were obsessed with the idea of making a flying machine. They spent hours and hours watching birds flap their wings, feeling the wind on their faces, and dreaming about zooming through the clouds. Then, one day, BAM! They had a genius idea: let's build our own airplane!

So, the brothers got busy in their wacky workshop filled with bicycles and gadgets. Despite facing many challenges, they tried all sorts of wing shapes and propeller designs. But you know what? They didn't let that stop them. Every time they messed up, they learned something new, getting closer and closer to their dream.

Finally, after what felt like a bazillion tries, the brothers unveiled their masterpiece - a magical machine with wings and a roaring engine. They called it the "Wright Flyer," and boy, was it ready to rock the skies!

One frosty December morning in 1903, everyone in Kitty Hawk was excitedly buzzing. Orville hopped into the pilot's seat while Wilbur checked everything. Their buddies gathered around, holding their breath as the engine came to life.

Whoosh! Off went the Wright Flyer down the track, faster and faster, until whoosh! It took off into the air, defying gravity like a boss. Orville and Wilbur's faces lit up as they soared through the air for a whopping 12 seconds, covering 120 feet. It might've been a short flight, but it was a HUGE deal - the first time people flew in a machine they'd built themselves!

The brothers hugged tight, grinning from ear to ear. Their dream had finally come true! And guess what? From that day on, everything changed. The Wright Brothers' incredible flying machine inspired loads of other folks to dream big and aim for the stars.

So, remember, kiddos: with a pinch of magic and a whole lot of determination, you can soar higher than you ever imagined!

Quiz

- Who were the two brothers who dreamed of flying in the small town of Kitty Hawk?

- What inspired Orville and Wilbur Wright to start building their own airplane?

- What challenges did Orville and Wilbur face while creating their flying machine?

- What was the name of the airplane the Wright brothers built, and what made it unique?

- How did the Wright brothers' first flight inspire others?

STORY 2:

What Mysteries Lie Within the Bermuda Triangle?

In the wide open sea, there's a spot where ships and planes vanish into thin air! It's called the Bermuda Triangle! Have you heard of it? Let's dive deep into the secrets of this mysterious place.

Imagine this: You're sailing across the Atlantic Ocean, enjoying the sunshine and salty breeze, when suddenly, your ship disappears without a trace! Spooky, right? Well, that's what some people say happens in the Bermuda Triangle.

So, where exactly is this Bermuda Triangle? Picture a triangle-shaped area with corners in Bermuda, Miami, and Puerto Rico. Within this triangle, strange things have been happening for years.

Legend has it that ships and planes just vanish into thin air within the Bermuda Triangle. But is it true? Scientists have been trying to crack the mystery for ages.

One theory is that wild weather might be to blame. Storms can whip up huge waves and strong winds, making it easy for ships and planes to get lost at sea. Imagine trying to find your way with rain pouring down and lightning flashing all around you!

Another idea is that the Bermuda Triangle has some funky magnetic stuff going on. Yep, you heard that right! Magnetic fields in this area might mess with compasses, making navigation difficult for sailors and pilots.

But wait, there's more! Some people think underwater volcanoes or bubbles of gas rising from the ocean floor could be causing ships to disappear. Imagine sailing along, minding your own business, when suddenly your boat gets sucked under by a giant bubble!

Despite all these theories, the Bermuda Triangle remains a mystery. But that hasn't stopped brave explorers from venturing into its waters to uncover the truth.

So, what do you think? Is the Bermuda Triangle just a spooky story, or is something mysterious lurking beneath the waves? It's up to you to decide!

As you ponder the secrets of the Bermuda Triangle, remember that the world is full of mysteries waiting to be solved. Who knows? Maybe you'll be the one to crack the case and uncover the truth behind this puzzling place!

And with that, we wrap up our adventure into the depths of the Bermuda Triangle. Until next time, keep your eyes peeled for more mysteries waiting to be discovered!

Quiz

- Where is the Bermuda Triangle located, and what shape does it form?

- What are some of the mysterious phenomena reported to happen within the Bermuda Triangle?

- What are some theories proposed to explain the disappearances of ships and planes in the Bermuda Triangle?

- How do wild weather conditions play a role in the Bermuda Triangle's mysteries?

- What message does the author leave with readers at the end of the exploration into the Bermuda Triangle?

STORY 3:

Did Felix Baumgartner Really Jump from Space?

In the wide-open skies above Earth, a thrilling adventure unfolded as a brave explorer named Felix Baumgartner aimed to jump from the edge of space!

Picture this: Felix, geared up in his special suit, ready to make history with the most daring leap ever attempted. But did he really jump from space, or is it just a tall tale?

Let's dive into the story! Felix's journey began when he boarded a giant balloon, like something from a fantastic storybook. This balloon carried him high up, nearly 24 miles above the ground. Can you imagine being that high? It's like flying with the birds, only much, much higher!

As Felix climbed higher and higher, the air around him got thinner, and the world below started to look like a tiny toy town. But he wasn't scared! With a heart full of courage, Felix stepped out into the vastness of space—or did he?

Here's the twist: Felix didn't exactly jump from outer space. He leaped from the very edge of our atmosphere, where space begins. It's like standing on the edge of a super tall cliff, but instead of falling, you fall straight out into the sky!

But wait, there's more to this amazing adventure! As Felix zoomed back to Earth at super speed, he didn't just fall like a stone. Oh no! He soared like a superhero, slicing through the air with style and grace. It's almost like he had wings!

The world watched in awe as Felix descended, his parachute billowing like a giant colorful umbrella. With a gentle touchdown, Felix landed safely on the ground, proving that even the wildest dreams can come true with a bit of bravery and determination.

So, did Felix Baumgartner jump from space? Well, not exactly. But his incredible leap from the edge of our atmosphere showed us that the sky's the limit when it comes to exploring the great unknown. Who knows what other amazing adventures await us among the stars?

Quiz

- What was Felix Baumgartner's daring mission?

- How high did Felix ascend before his jump?

- What did Felix experience as he climbed higher into the sky?

- Did Felix actually jump from outer space?

- How did Felix's incredible leap inspire others to dream big and explore the unknown?

STORY 4:

Who Was the Mysterious Red Baron of the Skies?

In the wild skies of World War I, there was one pilot who was feared by enemies and cheered by friends – Manfred von Richthofen, better known as the Red Baron. With his flashy red plane and fantastic flying skills, he became a superstar of the skies!

Born in a fancy Prussian family in 1892, Manfred had a thing for flying right from the start. He joined the German Air Force, called the Luftstreitkräfte, in 1915 and quickly showed everyone how awesome he was at flying.

Before you knew it, Manfred's plane was painted all red, earning him the cool nickname "Red Baron."

His bright red plane was like a warning sign to other pilots – it meant trouble was coming if they crossed paths with the Red Baron!

During his time in the sky, the Red Baron scored a crazy number of wins – he took down 80 enemy planes! How did he do it? He had super quick reflexes, awesome tactics, and was a total sharpshooter.

But the Red Baron wasn't just good at flying but also a super nice guy. Even amid intense dogfights, he stuck to his rules of being respectful and fair to his opponents.

Sadly, the Red Baron's impressive flying career ended on April 21, 1918, when he was shot down during a fight over France. People on both sides of the war were sad to hear about his passing, and he was given a big military send-off.

Even though he's not around anymore, the Red Baron's legend lives on! He's still inspiring pilots and wowing people worldwide with his crazy flying skills.

The Red Baron might be gone, but he'll never be forgotten!

Quiz

- Who was the Red Baron, and why was he famous?

- What was special about the Red Baron's plane?

- How many enemy planes did the Red Baron shoot down during his flying career?

- What made the Red Baron not only skilled but also respected by his opponents?

- How did the Red Baron's flying career come to an end?

STORY 5:

What Happened to MH370?

Once upon a time, in the vast blue skies above, there was a mighty airplane called MH370. It was no ordinary plane; it was a massive Boeing 777, ready to carry passengers on a thrilling journey from Malaysia to China. But little did anyone know, this flight would become one of the greatest mysteries of our time!

It was a beautiful day, the sun shining bright, as MH370 took off from Kuala Lumpur International Airport. Passengers settled into their seats, excited for the adventure ahead. But as the hours passed, something strange happened. MH370 vanished from the radar, disappearing without a trace! Where did it go? Nobody knew!

As days turned weeks and weeks into months, the world searched high and low for MH370. Ships scoured the oceans, planes flew overhead, and satellites scanned the skies, but there was no sign of the missing plane. It was like looking for a needle in a haystack!

But wait, here's where the mystery gets even more puzzling: Despite all the searching, nobody knows what happened to MH370. Some people think it might have crashed into the ocean, while others believe it was hijacked. There are even theories about aliens and secret government plots! It's a real-life whodunit, and everyone's got a different idea of what happened.

As the years went by, the mystery of MH370 captured the imaginations of people all around the world. Books were written, documentaries were made, and experts debated endlessly about what might have happened. But to this day, the fate of MH370 remains one of the greatest mysteries in aviation history.

So, what do you think happened to MH370? Did the ocean swallow it up? Spirited away by aliens? Or maybe it's hiding out on a secret island, waiting to be discovered! Whatever the truth, the mystery of MH370 will continue to intrigue and fascinate us for years to come.

Quiz

- What kind of airplane was MH370, and where was it headed?

- What happened to MH370 shortly after it took off?

- How did the world respond to the disappearance of MH370?

- What are some of the theories about what might have happened to MH370?

- Why is the mystery of MH370 considered one of the greatest in aviation history?

STORY 6:

Did Amelia Earhart Fly Solo Across the Atlantic in 1932?

In the awesome year of 1932, all eyes were glued to the sky as a super-brave pilot named Amelia Earhart geared up for a wild adventure that would go down in history books.

Amelia had a dream – she wanted to be the very first gal to fly solo across the gigantic Atlantic Ocean, something nobody like her had ever done before. She set off on her epic journey with a heart full of bravery and eyes sparkling with determination.

It's May 20, 1932, and the sun is shining bright as can be. Amelia hops into her trusty airplane, a snazzy red Lockheed Vega. Dressed up in her flying gear and goggles snugly in place, she waves goodbye to the cheering crowd gathered to watch her make history. The engine roars like a lion as she rolls down the runway, ready to take on whatever comes her way.

For what seems like forever, Amelia zooms through the sky, eyes locked on the horizon, focused on her big goal. Down below, the ocean stretches like a massive blue carpet, endless and a little scary. But Amelia? She's not scared one bit. She's on a mission to show everyone that girls can rule the skies just as well as boys.

As time passes, Amelia faces all sorts of tricky challenges - crazy winds, puffy clouds, and the nagging worry of running out of fuel. But does she give up? Nope, not a chance! She's got her eyes on the prize, and nothing's going to stop her.

Finally, after a whopping 14 hours of nonstop flying, Amelia's plane bursts through the clouds, and there it is - the rocky coastline of Ireland. Tears of pure joy stream down her face as she realizes she's done it - she's the very first lady to fly solo across the Atlantic, no stopping!

Word of Amelia's incredible adventure spreads like wildfire, inspiring folks worldwide, whether boys or girls, to aim high and chase their dreams. Amelia Earhart didn't just make history; she showed the world what it means to follow your dreams, no matter how big they seem.

So, as Amelia lands her plane on the runway in Ireland, her heart is bursting with pride, and her eyes are shining brighter than the sun. She knows her daring solo flight across the Atlantic will go down in history as a super example of bravery, determination, and the wild spirit of adventure.

Quiz

- Who was Amelia Earhart, and what was her dream in 1932?

- Describe the scene on May 20, 1932, as Amelia prepared for her historic flight.

- What challenges did Amelia face during her solo flight across the Atlantic?

- How did Amelia feel when she finally reached Ireland's coastline?

- How did Amelia's solo flight inspire people around the world, regardless of gender?

STORY 7:

Who Will Win the Sky Battle: Britain or the Luftwaffe?

Hey there, history adventurers! Let's dive into a super cool story from way back in the summer of 1940 – the Battle of Britain! This epic showdown in the sky was like something out of a movie, with heroes, villains, and jaw-dropping action!

It's 1940, and Britain is in big trouble. The Royal Air Force (RAF) is up against the German Luftwaffe, and things are getting intense. This battle, known as the Battle of Britain, was a total game-changer, testing the bravery and strength of the British people like never before.

So, what's the deal? Well, Adolf Hitler and his buddies are on a mission to take over Europe, and Britain is the last place standing in their way. But the British folks aren't about to back down! The RAF is ready to take on the bad guys, led by their Prime Minister Winston Churchill and the super smart Air Chief Marshal Hugh Dowding.

From airfields all over southern England, brave pilots hop into their planes - the famous Spitfire and Hurricane aircraft - and zoom into the sky to face off against the German bombers and fighters. It's like a giant game of cat and mouse but way cooler!

These pilots go head-to-head in epic battles in the clouds every day. It's like something out of a superhero movie! Even though they're outnumbered and outgunned, the RAF pilots never give up. They fight with everything they've got, showing off their amazing skills and tons of courage.

And guess what? Their hard work pays off! They give the Luftwaffe a run for their money, forcing Hitler to rethink his invasion plans. Pretty awesome, right?

But the battle isn't over yet! In September 1940, the Luftwaffe started bombing British cities, including the famous city of London, in what's called the Blitz. It's a scary time for everyone, but the British stay strong and keep fighting.

In the end, the RAF comes out on top! They defend Britain's skies like total bosses, showing the world that courage and determination can beat even the toughest odds. The Battle of Britain was a huge win for the good guys, giving them confidence and proving they would never give in to bad guys like Hitler.

So, let's give a big cheer to the brave RAF pilots and all the awesome people who helped defend Britain during this epic battle. They're the real heroes of this amazing story!

Quiz

- What was the Battle of Britain, and when did it take place?

- Who were the key figures leading Britain during the Battle of Britain?

- Describe the aircraft used by the RAF during the Battle of Britain.

- How did the RAF pilots demonstrate courage and determination during the battle?

- What impact did the Battle of Britain have on the outcome of World War II?

STORY 8:

Who Were the Courageous Tuskegee Airmen?

Hey there, history adventurers! Let's take a trip back to the difficult days of World War II and meet some seriously cool heroes – the Tuskegee Airmen! These guys were like superheroes, breaking barriers and showing the world what they were made of!

It's the middle of World War II, and things are intense. But amid all the chaos, a bunch of brave guys from Tuskegee, Alabama, decided to do something amazing – become the first African American military pilots in the US Armed Forces! How awesome is that?

Even though they faced a ton of unfair treatment and prejudice, these guys never backed down. They were determined to show everyone they had what it takes to be top-notch pilots.

Under the guidance of some super dedicated instructors, the Tuskegee Airmen trained like crazy, learning all the ins and outs of flying and combat. And let me tell you, they were total pros at it!

In 1943, the first group of Tuskegee Airmen called the 99th Fighter Squadron, was sent off to North Africa. From there, they soared through the skies, showing off their skills and taking on the bad guys like bosses!

Whether flying over North Africa's deserts or Europe's skies, these heroes were always ready for action. Even when some people doubted them because of their race, they never lost sight of their mission – to protect their country and defeat the enemy!

One of their coolest moments came in 1945 when the 332nd Fighter Group, also known as the "Red

Tails" because of the awesome red markings on their planes, pulled off a super daring mission. They escorted bombers deep into enemy territory, and guess what? They rocked it! Not a single bomber was lost, thanks to the skill and bravery of the Tuskegee Airmen!

These guys didn't just fly planes; they made history! They earned tons of awards and even helped change how people thought about race and equality in America. Talk about real-life superheroes!

Their legacy reminds us that no matter what obstacles you face, you can achieve anything with talent and determination. The Tuskegee Airmen will always be remembered as true American heroes who showed the world what it means to be brave and unstoppable!

Quiz

- Who were the Tuskegee Airmen, and what made them unique during World War II?

- Where were the Tuskegee Airmen trained, and what challenges did they face?

- What was the significance of the 99th Fighter Squadron and the 332nd Fighter Group?

- How did the Tuskegee Airmen contribute to the war effort in North Africa and Europe?

- What impact did the Tuskegee Airmen have on racial equality and perceptions in America?

STORY 9:

Can Chuck Yeager Break the Sound Barrier?

Hey there, future aviators! Get ready to zoom back into the super cool post-World War II era, where aviation was taking off like never before! And guess who's leading the charge? None other than the amazing Chuck Yeager – a pilot with nerves of steel and a heart full of sky-high dreams!

It's 1947, and Chuck Yeager is about to make history in the coolest way possible. He's strapping himself into the cockpit of the Bell X-1 – a super sleek, super powerful plane built to break the sound barrier. That's right – Chuck's about to fly faster than the speed of sound, and everyone's holding their breath to see if he can pull it off!

Chuck feels the adrenaline pumping through his veins as the X-1 gets hitched to a B-29 bomber and zooms into the sky. But he's not scared - he's pumped! With a roar like thunder, he blasts off into the wild blue yonder, leaving ordinary planes in the dust.

As Chuck zooms faster and faster, something crazy happens - the air around him starts to shake, and there's this crazy roar. It's like nothing he's ever heard before! But Chuck's not backing down - he's pushing harder, faster, determined to break through that invisible barrier.

And then, boom! Chuck bursts through the sound barrier like a superhero breaking through a brick wall in the blink of an eye. He's flying faster than the speed of sound, and the whole world's cheering him on!

This epic moment isn't just cool - it's history in the making! Chuck Yeager's shown that supersonic flight isn't just a dream - it's real and awesome!

Thanks to Chuck's bravery, pilots and engineers everywhere are inspired to reach for the stars and push the limits of what's possible. He's a true hero of the skies, proving that you can soar to new heights and make the impossible possible with guts, determination, and passion!

So, here's to Chuck Yeager – the fearless flyer who showed us that the sky's not the limit – it's just the beginning of an amazing adventure!

Quiz

- Who was Chuck Yeager, and what historic event did he accomplish in 1947?

- What aircraft did Chuck Yeager fly to break the sound barrier, and how did he prepare for this daring feat?

- Describe the moment when Chuck Yeager broke through the sound barrier. What was the experience like for him?

- How did Chuck Yeager's achievement impact the field of aviation and inspire others?

- What qualities did Chuck Yeager demonstrate during his historic flight, and why is he considered a hero of the skies?

STORY 10:

Is the Concorde the Coolest Plane Ever?

Welcome aboard the journey of a lifetime, where we'll be soaring through the skies in the most legendary aircraft of all time – the Concorde! Get ready to buckle up and experience the thrill of supersonic travel like never before!

Back in the groovy era of the 1960s, when bell bottoms and disco ruled, something truly magical took flight – the Concorde! This super sleek and lightning-fast passenger plane was a total game-changer, zipping through the air faster than the speed of sound. Can you imagine zooming from New York to London in just three and a half hours? That's faster than you can say "supersonic!"

But the Concorde wasn't just about speed – oh no! It was all about luxury and style, too. Picture this: you're lounging in a spacious cabin, sipping fancy drinks and munching on gourmet goodies while the world whizzes below. Talk about living the high life!

Let's fast forward to 2003, when the curtain closed on the Concorde's incredible journey. Sure, it faced some bumps along the way, like pesky noise complaints and high costs, but it was pure magic for the lucky folks who got to ride in this sky-high marvel.

Even though the Concorde has retired its wings, its legacy symbolizes human innovation and daring adventure. It showed us that with a little imagination and determination, we could reach for the stars and achieve the impossible!

So, here's to the Concorde – the ultimate icon of air travel that will forever hold a special place in our hearts and inspire us to dream big, fly high, and reach for the sky!

Quiz

- What made the Concorde aircraft legendary, and what was its most remarkable feature?

- Describe the experience of flying on the Concorde during its heyday in the 1960s and 1970s.

- What led to the retirement of the Concorde in 2003, and what challenges did it face during its operational years?

- How did the Concorde leave a lasting legacy in the field of aviation despite its eventual retirement?

- Why is the Concorde remembered as a symbol of human innovation and daring adventure?

STORY 11:

Could Charles Lindbergh Fly Solo to Paris?

In the super-cool days of flying, one guy rocked the sky and stole everyone's hearts. His name? Charles Lindbergh! Back in 1927, he went on a crazy adventure that made him a total legend in the world of aviation.

It's May 20, 1927, and the sun is shining bright. Charles Lindbergh hops into his rad plane, the Spirit of St. Louis, at Roosevelt Field in New York. With cheers from the crowd, he revs up the engine, ready to do something everyone thought was impossible – fly solo all the way to Paris, France!

With a big wave, Charles zooms down the runway, his plane soaring into the sky. He's on a mission to conquer the massive Atlantic Ocean all by himself!

For hours and hours, Charles flies through the night, using the stars and moon to guide his way. It's just him, the endless ocean below, and the whoosh of the wind. It's scary, but Charles is determined to reach his goal.

As the sun starts to peek over the horizon, Charles spots the rugged shores of Ireland. Yay! He's getting closer to Paris! With a burst of energy, he keeps on flying towards the twinkling lights of the City of Light.

Then, as the sun sets on May 21, 1927, Charles sees Paris below him. Wow! He brings his plane down with a huge smile and lands at Le Bourget Field. He did it!

The whole world goes wild with excitement when they hear the news. Charles Lindbergh just pulled off the first-ever solo flight across the Atlantic! Not only did he make history, but he also inspired many people to dream big and reach for the sky.

So, next time you look up at the clouds, remember Charles Lindbergh and his extraordinary adventure. Who knows? Maybe you'll be the next sky hero!

Quiz

- What was the name of Charles Lindbergh's famous aircraft, and where did he embark on his historic solo flight?

- How did Lindbergh navigate during his solo flight across the Atlantic Ocean, especially during the nighttime hours?

- Describe Lindbergh's feelings and experiences as he approached the shores of Ireland and later Paris.

- How did Lindbergh's solo flight across the Atlantic Ocean impact the world of aviation and inspire others?

- What message does Lindbergh's story convey to aspiring aviators and dreamers?

STORY 12:

Who Won the Race to Space?

In the thrilling times of the Cold War, two big countries, the United States and the Soviet Union, got into a super exciting competition called the Space Race! It was like a big race in space, and everyone was cheering on!

It all started in 1957 when the Soviet Union launched something super cool called Sputnik 1. It was the first-ever man-made satellite to go around the Earth! This amazed everyone in the United States and made it a bit competitive. They wanted to show they could do amazing things in space, too!

So, the United States and the Soviet Union kept sending all sorts of spaceships and astronauts up there, trying to be the first to do all kinds of cool stuff.

The Soviet Union was the first to send a human, Yuri Gagarin, into space in 1961. He went around the Earth in a spaceship called Vostok 1. That was a huge deal!

But guess what? The United States had a big moment, too! In 1969, a super brave astronaut named Neil Armstrong stepped onto the moon's surface. He was the first person EVER to walk on the moon! He even said a famous line: "That's one small step for man, one giant leap for mankind." Everyone cheered and felt so proud!

That Moon landing was like winning a gold medal in the Space Race! It showed that people can do incredible things when they work together and never give up. After that, both countries kept exploring space, making amazing spaceships like the Space Shuttle and building the International Space Station. They even sent robots to other planets!

Even though the Space Race is over, its spirit lives on. It reminds us to keep dreaming big and exploring the unknown. Who knows what incredible adventures lie ahead as we reach for the stars?

Quiz

- What event marked the beginning of the Space Race, and which country achieved this milestone first?

- Who was the first human to journey into space, and what was the name of the spacecraft he traveled in?

- Describe Neil Armstrong's historic achievement in 1969 and what famous line he made upon stepping onto the moon's surface.

- How did Neil Armstrong's moon landing impact the perception of space exploration and the Space Race competition?

- What legacy does the Space Race leave behind, and how does it inspire future generations to continue exploring space?

STORY 13:

Was Laika the First Pup in Space?

Once upon a time, in a galaxy far, far away (okay, maybe not that far), there lived a very special dog named Laika. Laika wasn't just any ordinary pup – she was brave, adventurous, and had dreams that were out of this world!

Laika's story began in the groovy 1950s when humans were buzzing with excitement about exploring outer space. But there was one problem – they needed someone to test out the space rockets before sending astronauts up there. And guess who volunteered for the job? That's right – our fearless furry friend, Laika!

Now, you might be wondering, how did a doggo become an astronaut? Well, it all started when Laika was chosen for a super cool mission by some clever scientists in the Soviet Union. They built a special spacecraft just for her, called Sputnik 2, and Laika was chosen to be its very first passenger!

On the big day of the launch, Laika wagged her tail with excitement as she hopped into her cozy spacecraft. With a bark of determination, she was ready to embark on the adventure of a lifetime – to become the first dog in space!

As the countdown began, Laika's heart raced with anticipation. Five... four... three... two... one... and liftoff! The rocket blasted off into the starry sky, leaving Earth behind in a cloud of stardust. Laika's tail wagged furiously as she zoomed through the atmosphere, feeling weightless and free.

For hours, Laika soared through space like a cosmic canine superhero, sniffing out new galaxies and chasing shooting stars. She gazed out the window at the breathtaking views of Earth below, feeling like the luckiest pup in the universe.

But as much as Laika was enjoying her space adventure, she knew there was important work to be done. She sniffed around her spacecraft, making sure everything was in tip-top shape and reporting back to mission control with her findings.

After a few days of orbiting the Earth, Laika's mission came to an end. But her bravery and spirit would be remembered forever. She may not have made it back home, but her journey paved the way for future space explorers and showed the world that anything is possible – even for a little dog with big dreams!

And so, as we gaze up at the stars twinkling in the night sky, we remember Laika – the fearless furry pioneer who dared to venture into the great unknown and inspire us all to reach for the stars!

Quiz

- Who was Laika, and what made her unique?

- What was the purpose of Laika's mission in space?

- How did Laika prepare for her journey into space?

- What were some of the experiences Laika had during her time in space?

- What was the significance of Laika's mission for space exploration?

STORY 14:

Did Yuri Gagarin Really Leave Earth?

In the early hours of April 12, 1961, something incredible happened! Imagine this: the whole world was holding its breath, waiting to see what would happen next. It was Yuri Gagarin, a brave astronaut from the Soviet Union, who was about to blast off into space. Can you believe it? He was going to be the first human ever to leave Earth and travel into space!

As the sun peeked over the horizon at the Baikonur Cosmodrome in Kazakhstan, Yuri climbed into his tiny spacecraft called Vostok 1. He must have felt so excited and a little nervous, too! With a wave goodbye, he sealed himself inside, ready for the adventure of a lifetime.

Then, with a mighty roar, the engines roared to life, and Vostok 1 shot into the sky like a fiery rocket! Yuri was zooming through space at a whopping 17,000 miles per hour! Can you imagine how fast that is? He looked out his window and saw the Earth far below, like a big blue marble in a sea of stars.

Yuri floated in space for nearly two hours, taking in the incredible sights around him. But then it was time to come back home. As Vostok 1 started its descent, things got a little hot! The spacecraft got super hot as it zoomed back into the Earth's atmosphere, but luckily, Yuri was safe inside.

Finally, after what must have felt like forever, Vostok 1 landed back on Earth. Yuri stepped out, and guess what? He was greeted by cheering crowds, and the whole world celebrated his amazing journey! He had made history, becoming the first person to travel to space and back.

Yuri Gagarin's journey wasn't just a big deal for science – it was a huge win for all of us dreamers out there! He showed us that with courage and determination, we can achieve anything, even if it seems impossible. So, let's keep dreaming big and reaching for the stars, just like Yuri did!

Quiz

- Who was Yuri Gagarin, and what remarkable event occurred on April 12, 1961?

- What was the name of the spacecraft Yuri Gagarin traveled in, and where did his journey into space begin?

- How fast was Vostok 1 traveling as it soared through space, and what did Yuri see when he looked out of his window?

- Describe the experience Yuri Gagarin had during his nearly two-hour journey in space.

- What was significant about Yuri Gagarin's return to Earth, and how was he celebrated upon his arrival?

STORY 15:

Did Neil Armstrong Really Walk on the Moon?

On a sunny day in July 1969, people all over the world huddled around their TVs, super excited! Why? Because something out-of-this-world was about to happen! Neil Armstrong, a brave astronaut, was getting ready to lead a super cool mission to the moon called Apollo 11.

Armstrong and his buddy, Buzz Aldrin, were zooming towards the moon in a tiny spaceship called Eagle. Inside, they felt a mix of nervousness and pure excitement as they prepared for what was coming next.

After a long journey through space, Eagle gently landed on the moon's surface. Armstrong, taking one small step, said those famous words, "That's one small step for man, one giant leap for mankind." Can you believe it? He was the first human to ever walk on the moon!

As Armstrong climbed down the ladder, his boots made special prints in the moon dust. It was like leaving a mark on history! Armstrong and Aldrin explored for hours, taking cool moon selfies, collecting rocks, and doing experiments.

They saw Earth hanging in the sky like a beautiful blue marble. They felt amazed by the vastness of space and how tiny our world looked from up there. Their adventure wasn't just about science; it was about showing what humans can do when they dream big!

Armstrong and his crew were cheered as heroes when they returned to Earth! Their names became famous worldwide. Their bravery inspired tons of kids to dream of becoming astronauts, too. Armstrong's moonwalk wasn't just a big step for humankind but a giant leap for our spirit of adventure! His footprints on the moon will always remind us to keep exploring and never stop dreaming!

Quiz

- What historic event occurred in July 1969 that had people all over the world glued to their TVs?

- Who were the astronauts on the Apollo 11 mission, and what was the name of the spacecraft they traveled in?

- What were Neil Armstrong's famous words as he took his first steps onto the moon's surface?

- Describe some of the activities Neil Armstrong and Buzz Aldrin did during their time exploring the moon.

- How did Neil Armstrong's moonwalk inspire people around the world, and what significance did it hold for humanity's spirit of adventure?

STORY 16:

What Really Happened to Amelia Earhart?

In the summer of 1937, something super strange happened in the sky! It was like a real-life mystery movie starring one of the coolest aviators ever, Amelia Earhart. She was already famous for her awesome flights, but this time, she wanted to do something even crazier – fly around the world!

So, with her buddy Fred Noonan as her co-pilot, they hopped into their super cool plane, the Lockheed Electra, and zoomed off into the blue yonder. But, wow, they faced many problems along the way! There were storms, engine troubles, and other scary stuff. But did that stop them? Nope! They were determined to make history!

But then, on July 2, 1937, something spooky happened. Earhart and Noonan just disappeared! Poof! Vanished into thin air somewhere over the big, big ocean. Imagine that! The whole world was scratching its head, wondering what happened.

Even today, nobody knows what went down. Did they run out of fuel and splash into the sea? Did they get kidnapped by pirates? Or maybe they found a secret island and lived there forever like real-life castaways!

The mystery of Amelia Earhart is like a puzzle that nobody can solve. That's what makes it so cool, right? Even though she's gone, her adventurous spirit inspires us to dream big and reach for the stars. Who knows? Maybe one day we'll unlock the secret of Amelia's wild sky adventure!

Quiz

- What was Amelia Earhart's ambitious goal in the summer of 1937, and who was her co-pilot?

- Describe some of the challenges Earhart and Noonan faced during their around-the-world flight.

- What mysterious event occurred on July 2, 1937, during Earhart and Noonan's flight?

- What are some theories about what might have happened to Earhart and Noonan after their disappearance?

- How does the mystery of Amelia Earhart's disappearance continue to inspire people today, and what lessons can we learn from her adventurous spirit?

STORY 17:

What Makes the SR-71 Blackbird So Legendary?

In the world of airplanes, there's one that stands out like a superhero among sidekicks – the Lockheed SR-71 Blackbird. This jet isn't just any ordinary plane; it's a flying legend that's faster than a speeding bullet and tougher than a superhero's armor. Let's take a closer look at what makes the Blackbird so special!

Back in the days of the Cold War, when spies and secret missions were all the rage, the SR-71 Blackbird was developed in tippy-top secret. Its design was like something out of a sci-fi movie, with a super cool shape and materials that could handle crazy high speeds and temperatures hotter than a summer day in the desert.

But what makes the Blackbird soar above the rest is its speed. We're talking about zooming through the sky faster than you can say "super-duper fast." This jet could fly so high and so fast that even the bad guys couldn't catch it – it was like it had its own invisibility cloak!

Now, the Blackbird wasn't just zipping around for fun; it had an important job – spying! Yep, you heard that right. It was like James Bond but in the sky. Equipped with fancy cameras and sensors, the Blackbird could take top-secret pictures from way up high, helping out the good guys by gathering important info.

And wow, did the Blackbird break some records! It zoomed higher and faster than any other plane before it, earning itself the title of the "fastest plane in the world." It was like the superhero of the skies, showing off its incredible powers for all to see.

Even though the Blackbird retired a while back, its legacy lives on. People still talk about its daring adventures and jaw-dropping speed. It's like the stuff of legends, reminding us that when humans put their minds to it, they can achieve truly amazing things.

The SR-71 Blackbird will always be remembered as the ultimate flying hero, soaring through history with style and swagger!

Quiz

- What sets the Lockheed SR-71 Blackbird apart from other airplanes?

- How was the SR-71 Blackbird used during the Cold War?

- What were some of the remarkable capabilities of the SR-71 Blackbird?

- How did the SR-71 Blackbird contribute to important missions during its operational years?

- Why is the SR-71 Blackbird considered a legendary aircraft, even after its retirement?

STORY 18:

Was the Spitfire World War II's Greatest Hero?

In World War II's heart, a hero soared through the skies – the Supermarine Spitfire!

A sleek, powerful plane with wings like a bird ready to take flight. Designed by the super-smart R.J. Mitchell, this beauty showed up in 1936, and wow, did it make heads turn!

Now, let's zoom into 1940, when things got tough during the Battle of Britain. German planes were zipping across the sky like angry bees, but guess who stood in their way? You got it – the Spitfire! With brave pilots behind the controls, these planes took on the enemy with daring maneuvers and a lot of courage.

Picture this: high above the green fields of England, Spitfires and German planes were locked in a dance of dogfights. It was like a thrilling aerial ballet, with the Spitfire showing off its fancy moves and firepower, making the bad guys think twice about messing with Britain.

But the Spitfire wasn't just a cool plane but a symbol of Britain's never-give-up spirit. People looked up to see those familiar wings and felt a surge of hope – like a superhero swooping in to save the day!

Even after the war ended, the Spitfire kept zooming through the skies, showing off its skills in air forces all over the globe. Its iconic design and top-notch performance made it a legend in aviation history, reminding us of the brave souls who flew it and the freedom they fought for.

Quiz

- Who designed the Supermarine Spitfire, and when did it first appear?

- How did the Spitfire contribute to the Battle of Britain during World War II?

- What made the Spitfire stand out from other planes during aerial combat?

- Why is the Spitfire considered a symbol of Britain's resilience during World War II?

- What is the legacy of the Spitfire in aviation history, even after the war ended?

STORY 19:

How Did Captain Sully Pull Off the Miracle on the Hudson?

On a chilly day in 2009, something incredible happened over the icy Hudson River in New York City. US Airways Flight 1549, flown by Captain Chesley "Sully" Sullenberger, faced a scary situation when both engines stopped working after takeoff. What came next was a super impressive act of skill, calmness, and bravery that people still talk about today as the "Miracle on the Hudson."

When Flight 1549 took off on its way to Charlotte, North Carolina, nobody expected the scary stuff that was about to go down. Right after takeoff, the airplane hit a bunch of birds, which caused both engines to stop working. With the plane quickly losing height and no working engines, Captain Sullenberger had to make a tough choice.

Even though things looked really bad, Captain Sullenberger stayed cool and focused. Drawing on all his years of flying experience, he made a super quick decision to try something risky – landing the plane on the Hudson River. No one had ever tried landing a big passenger plane like that on water before!

As Flight 1549 came down towards the cold river, Captain Sullenberger guided the plane with total skill. He carefully dodged buildings and stuff in the busy city. With super steady hands, he pulled off a perfect landing on the water.

Right after landing, everyone on the plane and the crew rushed to get out before the plane sank. Luckily, with the help of emergency teams and boats nearby, all 155 people on board got out safely. It was amazing – nobody got seriously hurt!

Captain Sully's brave landing impressed people all over the world. Everyone cheered him for being so brave and smart during a scary moment. His amazing landing showed how important it is for pilots to be experienced and well-trained.

The Miracle on the Hudson is still a story that makes us all feel hopeful. It's about being brave and working together when things get tough. Even in the hardest times, heroes like Captain Sully show us we can get through anything.

Quiz

- What was the "Miracle on the Hudson," and who was the pilot responsible for it?

- What caused US Airways Flight 1549 to face a dangerous situation shortly after takeoff?

- How did Captain Chesley "Sully" Sullenberger respond to the engine failure on Flight 1549?

- Describe the landing of Flight 1549 on the Hudson River and its aftermath.

- What impact did Captain Sully's actions during the "Miracle on the Hudson" have on aviation safety and public perception?

STORY 20:

Why Did the Hindenburg Airship Go Up in Flames?

In the spring of 1937, something terrible happened in the sky. Imagine a huge airship called the Hindenburg soaring through the clouds like a floating hotel. It was supposed to be a fancy way for people to travel from Germany to the United States. But then, disaster struck!

As the Hindenburg tried to land in New Jersey, it suddenly burst into flames! The airship, once grand and majestic, turned into a blazing inferno. People on board and those watching below could hardly believe their eyes.

Tragically, 36 people on the Hindenburg and one person on the ground lost their lives in the fire. It was a shocking moment that shook the whole world. Everyone wondered how such a terrible thing could happen.

After the disaster, investigators tried to figure out why it happened. They discovered that the Hindenburg was filled with hydrogen gas, which can easily catch fire. This made the flames spread quickly, destroying the airship in no time.

But from this tragedy came important changes. Instead of hydrogen, airships started using helium, a safer gas. And strict rules were put in place to make sure air travel was much safer in the future.

So, while the Hindenburg disaster was a sad event, it also taught us valuable lessons. It showed us the importance of safety in the sky and how we can make flying safer for everyone.

Quiz

- What was the Hindenburg, and what was its purpose?

- Describe the events that led to the disaster involving the Hindenburg.

- How many people lost their lives in the Hindenburg disaster, and what were the immediate consequences?

- What did investigators determine was the cause of the Hindenburg disaster?

- What changes were made to airship safety regulations following the Hindenburg disaster?

STORY 21:

Was the Enola Gay's Mission a Turning Point in History?

Hey there! Let's dive into a fascinating tale from history: the Enola Gay and the incredible mission it embarked on during World War II.

It's the summer of 1945, and the Enola Gay, a mighty B-29 bomber, is soaring through the skies. Its mission? Delivering a bomb called "Little Boy" to the city of Hiroshima in Japan.

Now, the Enola Gay isn't just any plane – it's named after its pilot's mom, Colonel Paul Tibbets. With a belly full of secrets, it takes off from Tinian Island, ready for its historic journey. The bomb it carries isn't just any bomb; it's a game-changer, marking the start of the nuclear age.

As the Enola Gay closes in on its target, tension mounts. At precisely 8:15 a.m., the bomb drops, lighting the sky with a blinding flash. The devastation is immense – entire neighborhoods vanish, leaving behind rubble and ash. Thousands perish instantly, and many more suffer from injuries and radiation.

The Enola Gay's mission speeds up the end of World War II but raises big questions about using such powerful weapons. Should they be used in war? And what about the long-term effects of nuclear weapons on our world?

Decades later, we're still talking about the Enola Gay's journey. It's a reminder of the Allied forces' bravery and the terrible cost of war. As we remember that fateful day in August 1945, let's reflect on the power of human invention and our ongoing quest for peace in a world shaped by the atomic bomb.

Quiz

- What was the Enola Gay's mission during World War II?

- Who was the pilot of the Enola Gay, and why was the plane named after his mother?

- Describe the impact of the bomb dropped by the Enola Gay on the city of Hiroshima.

- What questions does the Enola Gay's mission raise about the use of powerful weapons in war?

- How is the Enola Gay's mission remembered, and what does it symbolize in the context of history?

STORY 22:

Did the Space Shuttle Change Space Travel Forever?

In the big, wide space, something super cool happened: the Space Shuttle zoomed into action! This spaceship was like no other, designed to blast off like a rocket, circle the Earth like a champ, and land back down just like an airplane. It was about making space travel easier, cheaper, and more awesome!

On April 12, 1981, everyone's eyes were glued to the screen as the Space Shuttle Columbia soared up from Kennedy Space Center in Florida. It was the start of something big! Five different shuttles – Columbia, Challenger, Discovery, Atlantis, and Endeavour – took turns flying into space on tons of missions for the next thirty years. They carried brave astronauts, cool satellites, and tons of science experiments up there!

The Space Shuttle was a real game-changer in space exploration. It helped build the Hubble Space Telescope, the International Space Station, and all kinds of mind-blowing science experiments where gravity didn't matter. Plus, it was all about teamwork – astronauts from all over the world joined American crews on these epic space journeys.

But it wasn't always smooth sailing. There were tough times, like in 1986 when the Challenger shuttle sadly exploded right after takeoff, and in 2003 when the Columbia shuttle broke apart during its return to Earth. Both times, brave astronauts lost their lives.

Despite those sad moments, the Space Shuttle kept inspiring people to dream big and aim for the stars. Its missions taught us so much about space, and its legacy lives on in all the discoveries and adventures it made possible. Even though the shuttles have retired since 2011, their journeys into space will keep reminding us of the incredible things we can achieve when we set our sights high!

Quiz

- What made the Space Shuttle unique compared to other spacecraft?

- Can you name the five different shuttles that were part of the Space Shuttle program?

- What significant achievements were made possible by the Space Shuttle program?

- Despite its successes, what were some of the challenges and tragedies faced by the Space Shuttle program?

- How did the Space Shuttle program inspire people to dream big and explore the unknown?

STORY 23:

Where Did Flight 191 Go?

Once upon a time, there was a big, shiny airplane called Flight 191. It was just like any other airplane, except it had a mysterious story to tell. This story is about how Flight 191 took off on a sunny day but never reached its destination. Let's embark on an adventure to uncover the secrets of Flight 191!

Flight 191 was getting ready for a super fun trip. Lots of excited passengers boarded the plane, ready to soar through the sky. But as the plane zoomed down the runway, something strange happened. It started shaking and wobbling, making everyone nervous.

As Flight 191 soared into the clouds, things took a turn for the worse. Suddenly, there was a loud noise, and the plane started to tilt to one side. Passengers held onto their seats, feeling scared and confused. What was happening up there in the sky?

Then, disaster struck! Flight 191 began to lose control and plummeted towards the ground. People on the ground looked up in shock as the airplane disappeared. What happened to Flight 191? Where did it go?

As investigators looked for clues, they discovered that Flight 191 had a problem with one of its engines. It was like the airplane had lost its superpowers and couldn't fly properly. But why did the engine fail? That's the big mystery we need to solve!

Some people believe that Flight 191 encountered bad weather, like strong winds and thunderstorms, that made it hard to fly safely. Others think that maybe there was something wrong with the airplane itself. Could it have been a spooky curse or just a simple mistake?

Despite the mystery surrounding Flight 191, one thing is for sure - we'll never forget the brave passengers and crew who were on board that day.

Their memory reminds us to always stay safe and be careful when we fly.

So, what happened to Flight 191? It's a question that still keeps people wondering to this day. Maybe one day, we'll uncover the truth behind this puzzling aviation mystery!

Quiz

- What was unusual about Flight 191's journey compared to other flights?

- What events unfolded as Flight 191 took off and ascended into the sky?

- What was the main cause of Flight 191's tragic fate, according to investigators?

- What are some theories or speculations regarding the mysterious circumstances surrounding Flight 191?

- What message does the story of Flight 191 convey to readers about aviation safety and remembrance?

STUART AKOLI

STORY 24:

Did Voyager Really Circle the Globe Without a Break?

In the big book of flying adventures, there's a chapter about a special plane called Voyager. It's a story filled with bravery, smarts, and a whole lot of daring!

Back in 1986, two amazing pilots, Dick Rutan and Jeana Yeager, hopped into Voyager and decided to do something wild – fly around the world without stopping or refueling!

On a sunny day in December, Voyager zoomed into the sky from Edwards Air Force Base in California. It was packed with everything it needed for the long journey ahead. Dick and Jeana were ready to take on the challenge, even though it meant flying for nine whole days and nights!

As they soared over oceans and continents, facing bumps and twists along the way, people all over the globe held their breath, cheering Voyager on. With each passing moment, Dick and Jeana got closer to their dream of being the first to complete this epic journey.

Then, on December 23, 1986, Voyager swooped back down to Edwards Air Force Base, completing its incredible adventure. Dick and Jeana emerged from the cockpit as heroes, celebrated for their bravery and skill.

Voyager's flight wasn't just about flying around the world – it showed everyone what amazing things we can achieve when we believe in ourselves and never give up. It's a story that reminds us to reach for the stars and never stop dreaming!

Quiz

- What was the daring challenge that Dick Rutan and Jeana Yeager embarked on in Voyager?

- Where did Voyager take off from, and what was its destination?

- How long did it take for Voyager to complete its journey around the world?

- What were some of the challenges that Dick and Jeana faced during their flight?

- What message does the story of Voyager convey about perseverance and achieving dreams?

STORY 25:

Was the Vought F4U Corsair the Hero of the Skies?

Amid the stormy skies of World War II and the Korean War, one plane soared above the rest – the Vought F4U Corsair! With its cool gull-wing shape and super strength, the Corsair became a total superstar in the history of fighter planes.

In 1940, the Corsair sprang into action, ready to defeat the bad guys in World War II. With its super-strong Pratt & Whitney engine and cool weapons, it became a real hero in the battles of the Pacific.

But what made the Corsair stand out was its funky gull-wing design. Picture a bird's wings swooping down – that's exactly how the Corsair's wings looked!

And guess what? This cool shape helped it zip through the air like lightning, making it a top pick for pilots.

Speaking of pilots, one name that rings loud and proud is Major Gregory "Pappy" Boyington. Leading the fearless "Black Sheep Squadron," Pappy and his Corsair crew rocked the Pacific skies, showing the bad guys who's boss!

Even after World War II, the Corsair kept rocking in the Korean War. It swooped down on enemy targets like a superhero, proving its strength and reliability in the toughest missions.

Today, the F4U Corsair isn't just a plane – it's a symbol of bravery and skill. Aviation fans still geek out over its awesome design and epic history, reminding us of the daring pilots who ruled the skies and defended freedom with every flight!

Quiz

- What made the Vought F4U Corsair stand out among other fighter planes during World War II?

- How did the Corsair's gull-wing design contribute to its performance in the air?

- Who was Major Gregory "Pappy" Boyington, and what was his role in relation to the Corsair?

- In which battles and wars did the Corsair prove its effectiveness as a fighter plane?

- What is the significance of the F4U Corsair in aviation history, even after its active service?

STORY 26:

Was the Doolittle Raid the Turning Point America Needed?

In the aftermath of the big surprise at Pearl Harbor, America had a big idea to hit back at Japan and show them what we're made of! Leading this brave charge was Lieutenant Colonel James Doolittle, a fearless flyer with nerves of steel and a heart full of courage.

On April 18, 1942, sixteen B-25 Mitchell bombers took off from the USS Hornet, zooming toward Japan like soaring eagles on a secret mission. The plan? Surprise the socks off Japan by bombing Tokyo and other important cities, proving we weren't about to let them get away with attacking us!

Despite facing huge challenges and scary odds, the brave crews of the Doolittle Raid kept on going, driven by duty and a strong determination to fight for freedom. They zoomed low and fast over enemy territory, dodging Japanese defenses and hitting their targets with bull's-eye accuracy.

The Doolittle Raid caught Japan off guard, leaving them shaking in their boots and giving American spirits a big boost when we needed it. Even though the damage wasn't huge, the raid showed Japan that American air power was nothing to mess with!

For Lieutenant Colonel James Doolittle and his fearless crews, the Doolittle Raid was like winning a big prize – a victory of brains, courage, and daring. It proved how determined Americans were to defend freedom and democracy, no matter what.

Even though some planes were lost, and brave crew members were hurt or captured, the Doolittle Raid will always be remembered for the incredible bravery and sacrifice of everyone involved. It's a shining example of American bravery and sticking to your guns, inspiring us all to aim high and never give up on what's right!

Quiz

- Who was Lieutenant Colonel James Doolittle, and what was his role in the Doolittle Raid?

- Describe the objectives of the Doolittle Raid and its significance in the context of World War II.

- How did the crews of the B-25 Mitchell bombers overcome challenges and execute the Doolittle Raid?

- What impact did the Doolittle Raid have on Japan and American morale during World War II?

- What enduring legacy does the Doolittle Raid leave in terms of American bravery and commitment to defending freedom?

STORY 27:

Can the Sun Power a Plane?

Once upon a sunny day, a marvelous invention called Solar Impulse took flight into the big blue sky. Imagine a plane powered not by noisy engines but by the sun's gentle rays! Yes, you heard that right! Solar Impulse was like a bright, shiny bird soaring high above the clouds, spreading its wings of innovation and hope for a cleaner, greener future.

With its sleek, shiny wings covered in solar panels, Solar Impulse was a true marvel of modern engineering. It could harness the sun's energy during the day to power its electric motors and even store some energy for flying at night. It was like having a never-ending supply of sunlight to fuel its journey through the sky!

But Solar Impulse wasn't just any ordinary plane; it was on a mission to show the world what could be achieved with renewable energy and clean technology. Piloted by brave adventurers Bertrand Piccard and André Borschberg, Solar Impulse embarked on an epic around-the-world flight, stopping in far-off lands and spreading its message of sustainability and innovation wherever it went.

As Solar Impulse soared across oceans and continents, it captured the hearts and imaginations of people everywhere. Children looked up at the sky and dreamed of a future where planes could fly without polluting the air and where clean energy could power our world without harming the planet.

And just like a superhero with a cape made of sunlight, Solar Impulse proved that the sun's power could take us to new heights. It showed us that with a little imagination and a lot of determination, we could create a brighter, cleaner, and more sustainable future for generations to come.

So, the next time you look up at the sky and see the sun shining down, remember the incredible journey of Solar Impulse—a flying machine powered by the sun's rays and fueled by the dreams of a better tomorrow. Who knows what other amazing adventures await us in the endless blue skies above?

Quiz

- What makes Solar Impulse unique compared to traditional airplanes?

- Who were the pilots of Solar Impulse, and what was their mission?

- How does Solar Impulse harness the power of the sun to fly?

- What message did Solar Impulse aim to spread during its around-the-world flight?

- How did Solar Impulse inspire people to envision a cleaner and more sustainable future?

One

STORY 28:

Do You Know What Makes the Boeing 747 So Legendary?

In the bustling world of airplanes, one giant reigns supreme: the Boeing 747! Imagine a massive flying castle whisking you away on adventures to far-off lands. That's the magic of the Boeing 747, also known as the "Queen of the Skies." Let's take a fun-filled journey into the sky and learn all about this amazing aircraft!

The Boeing 747 first took flight in 1969, spreading its majestic wings and soaring into the heavens. With its humpbacked design and four powerful engines, the 747 captured the hearts of travelers worldwide. But why do they call it the "Queen of the Skies"? Well, just like a queen rules over her kingdom, the 747 rules over the skies with grace and power!

Picture yourself stepping onto a Boeing 747. Inside, it's like a magical flying palace! There are rows and rows of comfy seats, big windows to gaze out of, and even cozy beds for long flights. It's like your own floating castle in the sky!

But wait, there's more! Did you know that the Boeing 747 has not one, not two, but THREE floors? That's right! The top deck is a special VIP area where lucky passengers enjoy extra space and luxury. It's like having your very own secret hideaway in the clouds!

Now, let's talk about those four mighty engines. They're like the heart and soul of the Boeing 747, pumping power and energy to keep it soaring through the sky. With all that strength, the 747 can fly for hours and hours, taking you to places you've only dreamed of.

But here's the coolest part: the Boeing 747 can carry tons and tons of stuff! From cars to cargo, even other airplanes – you name it, the 747 can carry it! It's like a flying superhero, swooping in to save the day with its super strength and enormous cargo space.

And get this – the Boeing 747 isn't just for passengers. It's also a superstar when it comes to flying goods all around the world. From fresh fruits to fancy gadgets, the 747 delivers everything you need right to your doorstep. It's like having your personal delivery dragon!

So, the next time you look up at the sky and see a big, beautiful Boeing 747 soaring overhead, remember why they call it the "Queen of the Skies." With its regal presence, incredible size, and endless adventures, the Boeing 747 truly is a majestic monarch ruling over the world of aviation!

Quiz

- What is the Boeing 747 commonly referred to as, and why?

- Describe the interior features of the Boeing 747.

- How many floors does the Boeing 747 have, and what is unique about the top deck?

- What role do the four engines play in the Boeing 747's performance?

- Besides carrying passengers, what other purposes can the Boeing 747 serve?

STORY 29:

Did the North American X-15 Soar to the Edge of Space?

In the exciting world of aviation, there's an aircraft that zoomed through the skies faster than a speeding bullet - it's called the North American X-15! This amazing rocket-powered plane was like something out of a superhero movie, leaving everyone amazed with its incredible speed and daring missions.

It's the 1960s, and space exploration is booming. Scientists and engineers are dreaming up wild ideas to push the boundaries of flight. That's where the North American X-15 comes in - a sleek, futuristic aircraft designed to soar higher and faster than any plane before.

The X-15 wasn't like your typical airplane. Instead of using jet engines, it used rocket power to blast through the atmosphere. With its shiny metal exterior and pointy nose, it looked like it was ready to blast off into outer space – and that's exactly what it did!

One of the coolest things about the X-15 was its speed. This baby could zoom through the sky faster than the blink of an eye, reaching mind-boggling speeds of over Mach 6 – that's six times the speed of sound! Can you imagine going that fast?

But wait, it gets even more awesome! The X-15 wasn't just fast – it was also super high-flying. It could soar up to the edge of space, where the air is so thin you could almost touch the stars. Pilots who flew the X-15 saw breathtaking views of Earth from way up high, where the sky turns from blue to black.

Now, you might be wondering, what did the X-15 do up there in the stratosphere? It was all about pushing the limits of what humans could achieve in flight. Scientists used the X-15 to study aerodynamics, space travel, and how pilots could handle flying at such incredible speeds.

One of the bravest pilots to ever fly the X-15 was a guy named Neil Armstrong –the same Neil Armstrong who later became the first person to walk on the moon! Before he made history in space, Armstrong was busy breaking records in the X-15, flying higher and faster than anyone had gone before.

The X-15 might have looked like something out of a sci-fi movie, but it was real – and it paved the way for the amazing spacecraft and airplanes we have today. So, the next time you look up at the sky and see a plane streaking by, think about the incredible adventures of the North American X-15, the rocket-powered marvel that soared to the stars and back!

Quiz

- What made the North American X-15 different from typical airplanes in terms of propulsion?

- How fast could the X-15 fly, and how does that compare to the speed of sound?

- Describe the altitude capabilities of the X-15.

- What were some of the purposes of the X-15 flights?

- Who was one of the famous pilots to fly the X-15, and what significant achievement did he later accomplish in space exploration?

STORY 30:

Could the Piper J-3 Cub Be Your Passport to the Clouds?

Once upon a time, in the magical world of aviation, there was a little plane called the Piper J-3 Cub. But don't let its small size fool you – this plane was a superstar in the sky!

Imagine a bright sunny day, fluffy clouds floating by, and you're sitting in the cockpit of the Piper J-3 Cub, ready for adventure. With its sleek design and shiny wings, this little plane was built for fun!

The Piper J-3 Cub first took flight way back in the 1930s. It was like a bird, soaring through the air with ease. Kids and grown-ups alike would watch in awe as it danced through the clouds, performing loops and rolls like a pro.

One of the best things about the Piper J-3 Cub was how easy it was to fly. Even beginners could hop into the cockpit and confidently take to the skies. It was like riding a bike, but it was way cooler!

But the Piper J-3 Cub wasn't just about flying high – it was also a great way to see the world below. You could spot sprawling fields, winding rivers, and even your house from high above! It was like having your magic carpet whisking you away on incredible adventures.

And let's not forget about the thrill of landing. With its trusty landing gear and a smooth touchdown, the Piper J-3 Cub made every landing feel like a grand finale. You'd touch down gently on the runway, feeling like a true ace pilot.

But what is the best part of flying the Piper J-3 Cub? The feeling of freedom. Up in the sky, you were king (or queen) of the world, with nothing but blue skies and endless possibilities ahead.

So, if you ever dream of soaring through the clouds, remember the Piper J-3 Cub. With its charm, grace, and sense of adventure, it's the perfect plane to take you on the ride of a lifetime!

Quiz

- When did the Piper J-3 Cub first take flight?

- What qualities made the Piper J-3 Cub easy to fly, especially for beginners?

- Describe the experience of flying the Piper J-3 Cub according to the passage.

- What were some notable features of the Piper J-3 Cub's design?

- How did flying the Piper J-3 Cub make people feel, according to the passage?

STORY 31:

Could Heroes in the Sky Save a City Below?

Once upon a time, in a faraway city called Berlin, there was a big problem. The city was split into two parts, East and West, by a big, gray wall. The people in West Berlin were stuck, and they needed help!

But who would come to their rescue? Cue the heroes of the Berlin Airlift! These weren't your typical superheroes in capes and masks – they were brave pilots flying big airplanes filled with goodies, like food, toys, and even chocolate!

The Berlin Airlift was like a giant air delivery service, but instead of packages, they delivered hope and happiness to the people below. The pilots would soar through the skies, dodging clouds and even sneaky bad guys, to ensure everyone in West Berlin had what they needed to stay strong.

The Berlin Airlift heroes would zoom over the city every day, dropping off supplies and ensuring no one was left behind. It was like a high-flying circus, with planes zooming in and out like acrobats in the sky!

But the Berlin Airlift wasn't all smooth flying. Sometimes, the weather would turn stormy, and the winds would blow the planes off course. And then there were those pesky "Soviet fighters" who would try to spoil the fun by causing trouble.

But did that stop our heroes? Not a chance! They were determined to keep the spirit of West Berlin soaring high, no matter what obstacles got in their way. With teamwork, courage, and a lot of heart, they showed the world that even the biggest walls couldn't keep kindness out.

As the days turned into weeks and the weeks into months, the Berlin Airlift heroes never gave up. And guess what? Their bravery paid off! The big, gray wall couldn't keep the people of Berlin apart forever.

Eventually, it came crashing down, and the city was united again.

The Berlin Airlift may be a story from the past, but its message of courage and compassion still flies high today. It reminds us that even when things seem tough, there's always a way to spread a little joy and make the world a brighter place – whether you're flying through the clouds or lending a helping hand on the ground.

So, the next time you look up at the sky and see a plane zooming by, think of the heroes of the Berlin Airlift and the incredible journey they took to bring hope to a city in need. Who knows? Maybe you'll be inspired to be a hero in your own way, too!

Quiz

- Where did the story of the Berlin Airlift take place?

- Who were the heroes of the Berlin Airlift, and what did they do?

- What challenges did the pilots face during the Berlin Airlift?

- How did the Berlin Airlift contribute to the eventual fall of the Berlin Wall?

- What message does the story of the Berlin Airlift convey?

STORY 32:

What Happened to the Brave Astronauts?

In 1986, the world held its breath as the Challenger space shuttle prepared to launch into the great unknown. Named after a magnificent ship that once sailed the seas, Challenger was more than just a spacecraft; it was a symbol of human ingenuity and exploration.

But on that fateful day in January, tragedy struck. As millions watched in anticipation, Challenger lifted off from the launch pad at Kennedy Space Center, carrying seven brave astronauts on a journey to the stars. Among them was Christa McAuliffe, a teacher who dreamed of inspiring her students from space.

As Challenger soared higher and higher into the sky, excitement filled the air. But just 73 seconds after liftoff, disaster struck. A plume of smoke billowed from the shuttle's boosters, and then, in an instant, Challenger exploded into a fireball, scattering debris across the sky.

The world watched in horror as the shuttle broke apart and the brave astronauts were lost. It was a heartbreaking moment, a reminder of the dangers of space exploration and the fragility of human life.

But even in the face of tragedy, the spirit of Challenger lived on. In the months and years that followed, NASA investigated the accident and made changes to ensure the safety of future missions. And though the loss of Challenger was a devastating blow, it served as a reminder of the importance of pushing the boundaries of exploration and discovery.

Today, the legacy of Challenger lives on in the hearts and minds of people worldwide. Its story serves as a reminder of the courage and sacrifice of those who dare to reach for the stars, and its memory inspires future generations to never stop dreaming of what lies beyond the horizon.

Challenger may have been lost, but its spirit lives on, a beacon of hope and inspiration for all who gaze up at the stars and wonder what lies beyond.

Quiz

- What was the Challenger space shuttle's mission in 1986?

- Who was among the crew of the Challenger space shuttle, and what was her profession?

- Describe the tragic event that occurred during Challenger's liftoff.

- How did the world react to the Challenger disaster?

- What actions did NASA take in response to the Challenger tragedy?

- What is the legacy of the Challenger space shuttle?

STORY 33:

Can You Solve the Mystery of Flight 19?

In the realm of aviation mysteries, few stories captivate the imagination, like the enigmatic disappearance of Flight 19. This tale, set amidst the mysterious waters of the Bermuda Triangle, has puzzled historians and adventurers for decades. Join us as we embark on a thrilling journey to uncover the secrets of Flight 19 and the legendary Bermuda Triangle!

It all began on a fateful December day in 1945, when five TBM Avenger torpedo bombers took off from Fort Lauderdale, Florida, for a routine training mission. Led by experienced flight instructor Lieutenant Charles Taylor, the crew of Flight 19 embarked on what should have been a straightforward exercise over the Atlantic Ocean.

But as the afternoon wore on, something strange happened. Communication with Flight 19 became sporadic and confused, with Lieutenant Taylor reporting compass malfunctions and difficulty navigating. Despite the efforts of ground control to guide them back to base, Flight 19 seemed lost in a sea of confusion.

As darkness fell and fuel ran low, the fate of Flight 19 became increasingly uncertain. Distress calls crackled over the radio, conveying a growing desperation among the crew. Then, suddenly, silence. Flight 19 vanished without a trace, leaving a mystery that would endure for generations.

In the aftermath of Flight 19's disappearance, extensive search efforts were launched to locate the missing aircraft and its crew. Despite scouring thousands of square miles of ocean, no sign of Flight 19 was ever found. The disappearance of the five bombers, along with the rescue aircraft sent to find them, remains one of the greatest mysteries in aviation history.

Numerous theories have been proposed to explain the disappearance of Flight 19, ranging from navigational errors to extraterrestrial encounters. Some speculate that the Bermuda Triangle, a notorious area known for unexplained disappearances, played a role in the fate of Flight 19. Others suggest more rational explanations, such as adverse weather conditions or mechanical failures.

Regardless of the cause, the mystery of Flight 19 continues to capture the imagination of adventurers and historians alike. The Bermuda Triangle, with its tales of vanished ships and aircraft, remains a source of fascination and intrigue, inviting explorers to uncover its secrets and unlock the mysteries of the deep.

As we delve into the mystery of Flight 19 and the Bermuda Triangle, one thing remains certain – the allure of the unknown will continue to beckon adventurers to the watery depths, where the secrets of Flight 19 may one day be revealed.

Quiz

- When did the mysterious disappearance of Flight 19 occur?

- Who was the flight instructor leading Flight 19, and what complications did he encounter during the mission?

- What happened as darkness fell and fuel ran low during Flight 19's mission?

- How did search efforts unfold in the aftermath of Flight 19's disappearance, and what were the outcomes?

- What are some of the theories proposed to explain the disappearance of Flight 19, including its possible connection to the Bermuda Triangle?

STORY 34:

Did Glenn Miller's Music Take a Secret Flight?

Buckle up, young adventurers, as we embark on a thrilling journey to uncover the mysterious disappearance of bandleader extraordinaire Glenn Miller!

Imagine it's December 1944, and World War II is raging across the globe. Glenn Miller, the maestro behind toe-tapping tunes like "In the Mood" and "String of Pearls," decides to spread musical cheer to troops stationed in France. So, he boards a plane headed for Paris, ready to serenade soldiers with his swingin' melodies and brighten their spirits.

But as the plane zooms over the English Channel, something strange happens – poof! It vanishes into thin air! ⚔ Where did it go? What caused this puzzling disappearance? Was it a case of mischievous clouds playing hide-and-seek, or could it be something more mysterious?

Despite frantic search efforts, Glenn Miller's plane is nowhere to be found. The world is left scratching its head: Where did the bandleader and his merry musicians vanish to? Some whisper tales of hidden treasure and secret missions, while others speculate about encounters with UFOs. The truth remains as elusive as a high note on a saxophone.

But fear not, intrepid explorers! Though Glenn Miller's final flight may be shrouded in mystery, his music lives on. His catchy tunes continue to get toes tapping and fingers snapping, proving that a melody can light up the darkest skies even in the face of uncertainty.

So, the next time you find yourself humming to "Tuxedo Junction" or "Little Brown Jug," remember the musical magician who disappeared into the clouds but left a legacy that will never fade away.

Quiz

- When did Glenn Miller embark on his fateful journey to Paris?

- What was Glenn Miller's profession, and what were some of his popular songs?

- What event occurred as Glenn Miller's plane flew over the English Channel?

- How did people react to Glenn Miller's disappearance, and what are some of the theories surrounding it?

- Despite the mystery surrounding Glenn Miller's disappearance, what aspect of his legacy endures?

STORY 35:

Did Aliens Really Visit Broad Haven?

Welcome to the charming village of Broad Haven in Wales, where some curious school kids stumbled upon an out-of-this-world surprise during their lunch break back in 1977. Picture this: it's a crisp February day, and the children are frolicking in the schoolyard when suddenly, they spot something super strange in the sky.

What was it, you ask? None other than a shiny, silver flying saucer hovering over a nearby field! Yep, you heard that right – a bona fide UFO right in their backyard! The kids couldn't believe their eyes as they watched the mysterious craft descend from the heavens, emitting funky lights and a mysterious hum.

Now, let's get to the juicy details. According to these brave little adventurers, the UFO was like something straight out of a sci-fi flick – round, with a big dome on top and glowing lights all around. But that's not all – they even claimed to have seen a figure inside the saucer, wearing a shiny silver suit! Talk about a close encounter of the coolest kind!

But hold on to your space helmets because that's just the beginning. Soon after the kids' jaw-dropping sighting, reports started flooding in from other folks in Broad Haven, all claiming to have seen similar strange things in the sky. Some spotted twinkling lights zipping across the heavens, while others claimed to have glimpsed weird creatures roaming the fields at night. It was like the village had turned into its very own UFO hotspot!

Now, you might be wondering, what on Earth (or maybe not on Earth!) could explain these bizarre sightings? Well, that's the million-dollar question! Despite investigations by the grown-ups and the experts, nobody could quite crack the case. Some said it might've been a case of mistaken identity – perhaps the kids saw a fancy weather balloon or a sneaky military aircraft. But others believed that maybe, just maybe, the children had stumbled upon visitors from a galaxy far, far away!

And so, the mystery of the Broad Haven Triangle was born – an area where UFO sightings and unexplained happenings left folks scratching their heads and looking to the stars for answers. Even though the truth may still be out there somewhere, one thing's for sure – the tale of the Broad Haven UFOs will forever remain a delightful slice of extraterrestrial excitement in the annals of Welsh history!

Quiz

- What did the school kids spot during their lunch break in Broad Haven?

- How did the children describe the appearance of the UFO they witnessed?

- What additional sightings were reported by other residents of Broad Haven after the school kids' initial UFO sighting?

- What were some of the explanations proposed by adults and experts to explain the mysterious sightings in Broad Haven?

- What nickname was given to the area where the UFO sightings occurred, and why?

CONCLUSION

As our journey through the skies comes to a close, we reflect on the incredible adventures we've shared and the remarkable stories we've uncovered. "Aviation Stories for Curious Kids" has taken us on a whirlwind tour of the history of flight, introducing us to brave pilots, groundbreaking aircraft, and mysterious phenomena that have captured the imagination for generations.

From the courageous solo flights of Amelia Earhart and Charles Lindbergh to the heroic missions of the Tuskegee Airmen and the daring space explorations of Yuri Gagarin and Neil Armstrong, we've witnessed the triumphs of human ingenuity and the relentless pursuit of exploration and discovery.

But our journey doesn't end here. As we close the final pages of this book, we're reminded that the sky is not the limit; it's just the beginning. There are still mysteries to unravel, challenges to overcome, and adventures yet to be had. Whether you dream of soaring through the clouds or reaching for the stars, remember the lessons and inspiration you've found within these pages.

So, let your curiosity take flight, young aviators, and never stop exploring the wonders of the world above. Who knows what new horizons await you as you spread your wings and soar into the future? The sky's the limit - and beyond!

Made in United States
Orlando, FL
12 November 2024